MARTIAL ARTS
JUDO

Raintree www.raintreepublishers.co.uk

To order:
Phone 44 (0) 1865 888112
Send a fax to 44 (0) 1865 314091
Visit the Raintree bookshop at
www.raintreepublishers.co.uk
to browse our catalogue and order online.

Produced by
David West ☆☆ Children's Books
7 Princeton Court
55 Felsham Road
London SW15 1AZ

Photographer: Bob Willingham
Designer: Gary Jeffrey
Editor: James Pickering

First published in Great Britain by
Raintree, Halley Court, Jordan Hill,
Oxford OX2 8EJ, part of Harcourt Education.
Raintree is a registered trademark of Harcourt
Education Ltd.

Printed and bound in Italy

ISBN 1 844 21691 8 (hardback)
07 06 05 04 03
10 9 8 7 6 5 4 3 2 1

ISBN 1 844 21696 9 (paperback)
08 07 06 05 04
10 9 8 7 6 5 4 3 2 1

British Library Cataloguing in Publication Data
Chesterman, Barnaby and Willingham, Bob
Judo. – (Martial Arts)
796.8'152
A full catalogue record for this book is available
from the British Library.

Acknowledgements
The publishers would like to thank the following for
permission to reproduce photographs:

Abbreviations: t-top, m-middle, b-bottom, r-right,
l-left, c-centre.

Cover, 6 all, 9l & b, 16b, 21tl, 24tl, 27tr & mr, 29
all, 30 all - Courtesy of Bob Willingham.

Every effort has been made to contact copyright
holders of any material reproduced in this book.
Any omissions will be rectified in subsequent
printings if notice is given to the publishers.

THE AUTHORS
Left – Barnaby
Chesterman, 1st
dan black belt and
official journalist of
The International
Judo Federation.

Right – Bob
Willingham, 4th dan black belt and official
photographer of The International Judo Federation.

THE MODELS Left to
right – Miles Goodman,
junior orange belt,
Carlos Thomas, junior
yellow belt, Jenny Richards, junior green belt.

Left to right – Jean-Rene
Badrick, junior brown belt,
Colleen Kerr, junior brown
belt, Robin Willingham, junior
white belt, Josh Shorlands, junior yellow belt.

*An explanation of Japanese judo terms can be
found on page 31.*

MARTIAL ARTS

JUDO

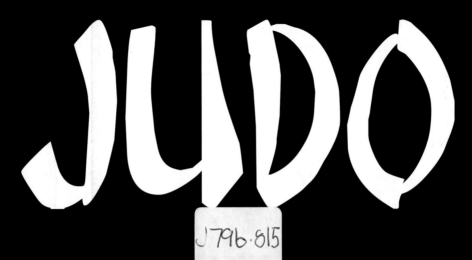

Barnaby Chesterman
Bob Willingham

Raintree

Contents

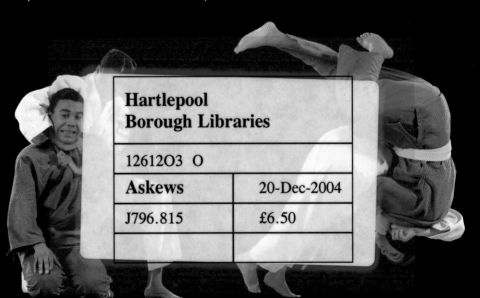

Introduction

Many people think of judo as a struggle between angry competitors in white pyjamas, tugging and bundling each other on to the floor. Nothing could be further from the truth. Judo is a dynamic and deeply spiritual martial art and Olympic sport. It requires agility, control and balance, so that the weak can overcome the strong and small people can topple bigger ones with breathtaking throws, holds or expert submission techniques.

History

The origins of judo, 'the gentle way', stem from the ancient Japanese martial art of ju-jitsu, 'the compliant way' – a form of open-handed, close-quarter combat that developed on medieval battlefields. The founder of judo was Jigoro Kano, a student of several forms of ju-jitsu. Born in a Japanese village in 1860, he adapted some of the techniques of ju-jitsu, and turned it into a sport and a form of self-defence. The

The founder of judo – Jigoro Kano

Yukio Tani was known as the pocket Hercules.

principle was to use minimal effort with maximum efficiency. He demonstrated this new, mysterious art in competitions all over the world. Early pioneers, such as Yukio Tani, became famous for incredible feats of strength – beating men who were much bigger and stronger. In 1964, judo became an official Olympic sport.

Anton Geesink (right), of the Netherlands, was the first Olympic judo champion in Tokyo, Japan in 1964. Although he had won the world championship three years earlier, the Japanese still expected to win Olympic gold.

Clothing & etiquette

Judo is steeped in ancient tradition. Even though it has developed into a modern combat sport, it still retains many of its medieval customs. Examples of this can be seen in the clothing and etiquette that are still used.

Judo clothing (judogi) consists of loose-fitting trousers and a thick open jacket, secured by a belt (obi), passed twice around the waist and tied at the front.

GRADING SYSTEM

Grades in judo are distinguished by different coloured belts.

10th *kyu*
9th *kyu*
7th–8th *kyu*
5th–6th *kyu*
3th–4th *kyu*
1st–2nd *kyu*
1st–11th *dan*

Junior grades are called *mon*, beginning with 1st up to 18th. Senior grades are called *kyu*, beginning with 10th up to 1st. Black belt grades have a special name – *dan* grades. The highest *dan* grade ever achieved was 11th by Jigoro Kano.

BOWING

Students of judo bow (*rei*) to show respect for the martial art, its founder Jigoro Kano, instructors and fellow students. Bowing is performed when entering and leaving a judo hall (the *dojo*), when stepping on and off the mat (the *tatami*) and before and after any practice or demonstration.

Judo elements

Judo has four main elements – throws, holds, armlocks and strangles. Students of judo learn all four, but juniors may not use armlocks and strangles in competition until they are 16 years old.

THROWS *(nage-waza)*

This is the most spectacular and dynamic element in judo. There are four categories of throws – hand techniques (*te-waza*), foot sweeps (*ashi-waza*), hip throws (*koshi-waza*) and sacrificial throws (*sutemi-waza*). Whichever techniques a fighter prefers, the aim is always the same – to throw an opponent flat on to his back with power and control.

HOLDS *(osaekomi-waza)*

Once two fighters collapse to the ground they move directly into groundwork. The aim here is to trap the opponent's shoulders to the mat and prevent him or her from escaping, by keeping your body weight balanced over his or her torso. This is called a hold-down.

ARMLOCKS
(kansetsu-waza)

The quickest way to gain victory is by a submission. Armlocks are submission techniques. By putting pressure against your opponent's elbow joint, you can force him or her to give up, by tapping.

STRANGLES
(shime-waza)

The other type of submission is the strangle. This is done by putting pressure against the side of an opponent's neck – cutting blood circulation, or across his throat – to stop him breathing.

Rules

As a physical combat sport, judo is regulated by many rules. A central referee and two corner judges enforce these rules.

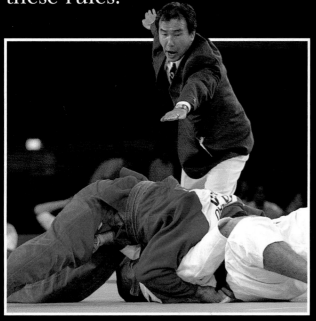

Referees have a range of arm actions to indicate scores given or decisions made.

PROHIBITED ACTS

Various moves or actions are forbidden in judo, punishable by a penalty score or disqualification.

Negative judo is where a fighter tries to hold his opponent off by locking his arms. In judo you must attack your opponent.

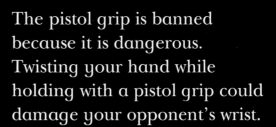

Holding one side of your opponent's jacket with both hands without attacking is not allowed for more than 3 seconds.

The pistol grip is banned because it is dangerous. Twisting your hand while holding with a pistol grip could damage your opponent's wrist.

Some dangerous offences, such as pushing your opponent's face or striking out in any way, result in outright disqualification.

SCORING

There are four types of judo scores, each of which has a penalty equivalent.

Ippon – this is a knock-out score and indicates immediate victory.

Waza-ari – this is a half point score, and two of these equal one *ippon*.

Yuko – this is a minor score and any number of these is still less than one *waza-ari*.

Koka – the lowest score. Any number will always be surpassed by one *yuko*.

A judo contest scoreboard

Breakfalls
(ukemi)

It is vital that you learn to fall without hurting yourself. There are four types of breakfall – front, side, back and rolling.

FRONT
Crouch down with your feet together. Throw your arms forwards and kick your legs out behind you, landing on your forearms and toes, with the rest of your body off the mat.

SIDE
From a crouching position, straighten your leg and topple to the side. Slap the mat with your arm straight, with fingers and toes pointing in the same direction.

ROLLING
Step forward with your left leg, and put your right forearm on the mat in front of you. Roll over your right shoulder and slap the mat with your left arm as you land. Now try it on the left hand side.

BACK
The back breakfall is needed when an opponent throws you directly backwards. Starting in a crouching position, kick your feet out in front as you fall backwards. As you land, slap the mat with both forearms, palms facing the mat.

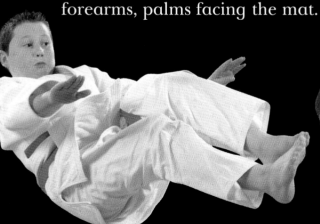

Evasions

You have learnt to fall safely, but the aim of judo is to win, so you don't want to be thrown. Now you must also learn how to avoid, block and twist away from throws.

Cartwheels are a good exercise to practise to avoid landing on your back. It's always best to keep your back off the mat!

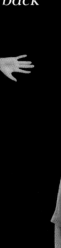

BLOCKING

This is a good exercise to counter hip throws. When your partner attacks with a hip throw, drop your hips, spread and bend your knees while wrapping your arms around his or her waist. Then push up with your hips and legs, lifting your partner off the mat.

BREAKING THE GRIP

As your partner turns in to attack, push your hips into his or her backside. Pull your arm free from his or her grip, as you turn your body away and step backwards.

TWISTING

Being able to twist out of a throw and land on your front is crucial. Practise this by getting your partner to hold your jacket as you lean backwards, keeping your legs straight. When he or she can no longer hold you and lets go, quickly twist on to your front as you fall.

Judo games

When you start learning judo, it's important to enjoy yourself. Judo games are fun, but they also teach you important skills. They can help improve your strength, stamina and mobility, while also fuelling your competitive spirit.

TUG OF WAR

This simple game builds up leg strength. Tie a belt between you and your partner, crouch down and start crawling!

MONKEY RUNS

In this game, both players have to work very hard. Two players take it in turns to crawl across the mat, with the partner hanging on beneath. To swap turns, don't let go of each other, just roll over!

MOBILITY JUMP

This is a test of explosiveness.

1 Three players line up close, ready to spring into action.

2 The middle player jumps left as the girl slides into the middle.

3 She jumps to her right.

ARM BOUNCE

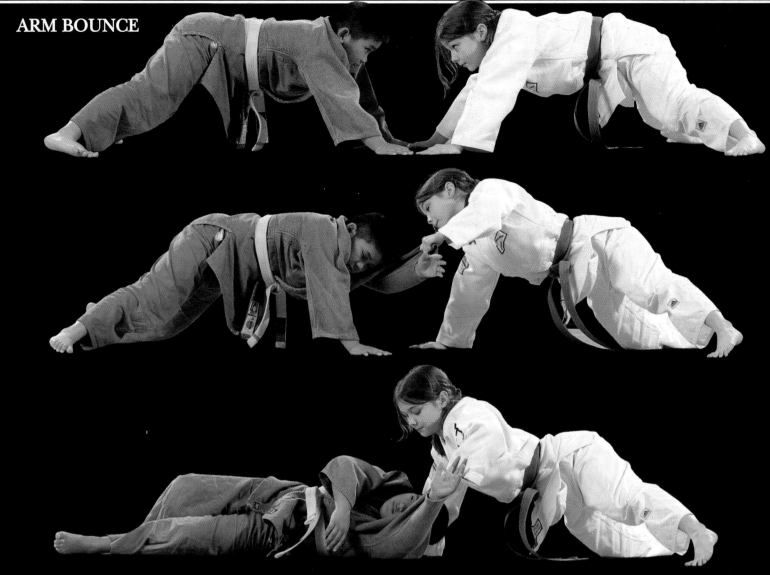

The arm bounce is about balance and strength under pressure. It teaches you to attack and defend together. Face up to your partner on your hands and feet, with your arms and legs spread out to give yourself balance. Supporting yourself on one arm at a time, try to break your partner's balance by tapping or pulling his or her arms away.

The boy slides in.

4 He jumps to his left to complete the sequence.

5 All three get ready to carry on – non-stop.

Training

As well as learning the basic elements of judo, you need to train your body. Judo is very physical and demanding, so you must be tough, but you must also develop a good technique. No matter how strong you are, someone with good timing and speed will be able to unbalance you.

Judoka practise grip fighting *(kumi-kata) to learn to dominate opponents physically.*

CRASH MAT RUNNING

This is a very energy-sapping exercise but it will build up strength and stamina in your legs. A lot of judo is done with the legs so they must be in good condition. Practise running on a crash mat, keeping your knees up and pumping your arms.

FLOOR EXERCISES

1 Fast squat-thrusts are good for your legs. **2** Star jumps are good for all round fitness and explosiveness. Try to jump as high as you can. **3** Sit-ups build up your stomach muscles. Do these slowly for greater effectiveness. **4** Press-ups give you strong arms, shoulders and chest. Do as many as you can, touching your chest to the mat each time.

TECHNIQUE PRACTICE
(uchi-komi)

The literal translation of *uchi-komi* is 'fitting in' (with each other). Take turns to practise your technique with the attacker (*tori*), throwing the defender (*uke*), who puts up only a little resistance. Make sure your technique and balance are good – don't pick up bad habits in *uchi-komi* as they are hard to lose later.

FREE PRACTICE
(randori)

This means 'catching chaos' and is the judo version of sparring. Partners attack each other as if they are in a contest situation. *Randori* is usually split into standing *randori* (using throwing techniques) and groundwork *randori* (using holds and submissions). But you can also include standing and groundwork in the same *randori*.

Groundwork randori

If you manage to throw both partners in explosive uchi-komi, *you can be certain your technique will work in competition!*

EXPLOSIVE *UCHI-KOMI*

Uchi-komi is good for practising your technique because your partner stands passively. But how will you know if your technique is really effective? In explosive *uchi-komi* you can practise at full speed and power, without hurting your partner. For this you need two *ukes* – one to be attacked and the other to hold him or her down.

Hand techniques
(te-waza)

This floating drop (uki-otoshi) is the ultimate hand technique.

Take hold of your partner's lapel with your right hand, and sleeve with your left – this is a conventional right-handed grip.

Pull your partner towards you as you step forward with your right foot, placing it just in front of his or her right foot.

Hand techniques have developed more than any other throwing method. Originally, the attacker (*tori*) used only momentum and a twist of the hands to send opponents flying through the air. But many of these required leg actions to become effective in modern competition. One of these is the body drop (*tai-otoshi*) which is one of the most effective competition throws.

In this body drop, Germany's Udo Quellmalz spreads his legs very wide, but the main impetus comes from his hands.

BODY DROP *(tai-otoshi)*

Swivel on the ball of your right foot as you step around and backwards with your left. Turn your body to face the same way as your partner and pull his or her sleeve.

Your partner will feel off balance and want to step forward with the right foot. Before he or she can, step across that foot, blocking the shin with your calf.

Rotate your arms, pushing up with your right and pulling down with your left. Straighten your right knee and your partner will tumble over your outstretched leg.

EVASION AND COUNTER ATTACK WITH INNER THIGH THROW *(uchi-mata)*

As your partner attacks with the body drop, start to move your hips to your right.

Lift your right foot and step over his or her throwing leg.

Place your foot out in front of your partner, as you slip your hips and left leg through.

As you bring your left leg through, sweep it inside your partner's right thigh.

Pull hard with your right hand and turn your head and shoulders.

Foot sweeps
(ashi-waza)

These are pure leg throws where you hook, sweep or block your opponent's foot or leg to throw him or her. These require great speed and timing.

ADVANCED FOOT SWEEP *(de-ashi-barai)*

A foot sweep whisks an opponent's feet from under him.

From a conventional right-hand grip, the aim is to force your opponent to take a step forward so that you can sweep her advancing foot. For this technique, you need to be very loose and relaxed.

Take a step backwards with your right foot as you pull your partner towards you. This forces her to take a step forward with her left foot to regain balance. You must catch this foot before it touches the mat.

EVASION AND COUNTER

The evasion and counter to the advanced foot sweep is both quick and subtle. You must dodge your partner's sweeping foot and catch it with a counter advanced foot sweep of your own, all in one swift movement.

Step over your partner's sweeping right foot before contact.

Before he can put it down, catch it with your own foot sweep.

Sweep through to your right and pull down with your left hand.

Just before your partner puts her weight on her foot, quickly step forwards with your right foot and hook her left ankle with your instep, as you lift her up on to her toes with your hands.

Continue to sweep your partner's left ankle away to your left as you drag her body down to your right with your hands. Her momentum takes her down to your right side, as she has nowhere to plant her weight.

Hip throws
(koshi-waza)

The hips and legs are very powerful weapons in judo. Hip throws, such as the hip wheel (*koshi-guruma*), are often the most dynamic and spectacular techniques.

With hip throws, push your hips across your partner's body and use the spring in your legs to launch him or her into the air. Turn your head and shoulders to throw your partner over your hip and on to his or her back.

HIP WHEEL
(koshi-guruma)

Hold your partner's lapel with your right hand and his sleeve with your left. Create a bit of space between the two of you, for you to move into when you attack.

Step between your partner's feet as you pull him close, by wrapping your arm around his neck. This secures his head and shoulders, giving you control of his torso.

A slight variation as Britain's Michelle Rogers spreads her legs and grips the lapel rather than the sleeve in a devastating throw.

BLOCK AND COUNTER

As this is a powerful throw, the evasion must be equally robust.

1 Spread your legs, bend your knees, and sink your hips lower than your partner's, as she turns in with her hip.

2 Gripping tightly around her waist, sit straight down and stretch out your left leg, taking her backwards over it with a 'valley drop' (*tani-otoshi*).

Bring your left foot next to your right and bend your knees. Pull hard on his sleeve as you turn your head and shoulders to the left, bringing your partner up on to his toes.

Straighten your legs and launch yourself forwards, rotating your head and shoulders to your left. Your partner somersaults over his own head and crashes down on to his back.

Sacrificial throw
(sutemi-waza)

This is the riskiest technique in judo, as you must throw yourself to the ground to topple your opponent.

STOMACH THROW *(tomoe-nage)*

As you will take your opponent directly over your head, you have a choice of grips, but the lapel-sleeve grip is always good.

Step in towards your partner with your left foot, and roll your fists upwards and towards you to ease your partner up on to his toes.

Bring your right foot up to his abdomen, placing the sole of your foot on the inside of his hip as you start to sit down.

Blocking the stomach throw is not difficult because you can easily slip past the attacking foot or push your hips into it to prevent your partner from straightening her leg. But to counter it you must have great anticipation.

Catch your partner's leg as the foot comes up to your waist.

Quickly hook the inside of her standing leg with a major inner sweep *(o-uchi-gari)*.

Follow your partner down to the mat by driving forward with your right hand.

Sit down almost on your partner's toes. Use the momentum of your falling body to pull his head towards the mat. Keep your leg straight and lever him off the ground over your head, keeping your hands close together.

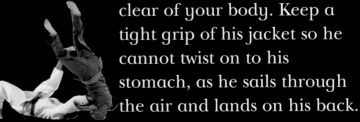

Keep pushing with your foot until your partner's momentum takes him over and clear of your body. Keep a tight grip of his jacket so he cannot twist on to his stomach, as he sails through the air and lands on his back.

Pinning techniques
(osaekomi-waza)

In a hold-down, you must secure your partner's shoulders and upper torso. Hold tightly, push your hips down and spread your legs.

Canada's Aminata Sall applies a variation of kata-gatame, *trapping her opponent's far arm across her face, rather than her near arm.*

The simplest way to end a contest on the ground is by pinning your partner on his or her back for 25 seconds with no means of escape. To do this, you must control your partner's shoulders, as in the shoulder hold (*kata-gatame*).

SHOULDER HOLD
(kata-gatame)

A common defence in groundwork is the 'turtle' position, where a fighter curls up into a ball. Control your partner by leaning your weight over him.

Slip your right arm under his right armpit and across his throat. You must do this quickly so he cannot see it coming or defend himself against it.

Take hold of your right hand with your left, and pull your partner in against your chest. Squeeze tightly to prevent him from attempting to crawl away.

Turn on to your right hip and reach over your partner's body with your left hand to grab hold of her belt.

Force your right hip under her body as you pull hard on her belt with your left hand.

As you roll her across your body, keep pulling on her belt and turn your hips and shoulders to your left.

Once she is on her back, slip your right arm back over her head and around her neck into a scarf hold (*kesa-gatame*).

Force your right knee underneath his body as you pull him up on to your right hip. Your knee will help lever him across your body and on to his back.

Lie flat as you roll your opponent across your body on to his back on your left-hand side. Use your momentum to rotate, and end up on top.

Push your partner's right arm across his face by leaning your head and shoulder into it. Perch up on your right knee, steadying yourself with your left leg.

Strangles
(shime-waza)

Strangles are one of the two types of submission technique. They can be applied with your arms or legs, or by using your partner's collar and lapels to choke him, as with the sliding collar choke (okuri-eri-jime).

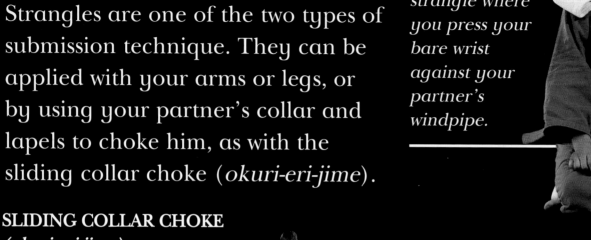

The naked choke (hadaka-jime) is a simple and effective strangle where you press your bare wrist against your partner's windpipe.

SLIDING COLLAR CHOKE
(okuri-eri-jime)

Some strangles can be done from in front of a partner, but the sliding collar must be approached from behind. If

your partner is defending on all fours, in the 'turtle' position, jump on his back and hook your legs under his body.

With your right hand under your partner's chin, and your wrist across his throat, tuck your thumb inside his lapel. Slip your left arm under his armpit and take hold of his opposite lapel and roll over.

DEFENCE

To defend a strangle you must stop it before it is applied. If you try to remove it once it is on, you will be too late.

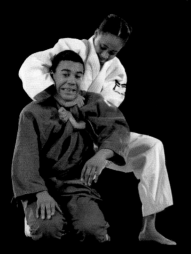

If your partner gets her wrist across your throat you are already too late and it will only be a matter of time before you submit.

Catch her wrist with your left hand before it's across your throat. Then pull down on her elbow with your right hand. This releases a gap around your neck.

Germany's Udo Quellmalz struggles to apply the sliding collar choke because he has the wrong lapel in his right hand.

North Korea's Chang Su Li wins against Marc Alexandre of France with a sliding collar choke.

Hook your right foot inside his right knee and roll to your left. Drive your left leg through the gap under his body and use your left arm to lever his left hand off the mat. Your partner will fall on to his left side.

Keep your legs tightly around your partner to stretch him out. Pull his lapel across his throat with your right hand as you pull down on his opposite lapel with your left hand. Try to straighten your elbows.

Armlocks
(kansetsu-waza)

The aim of an armlock is to put pressure against your partner's elbow joint, forcing her to submit.

Armlocks can be very painful as you try to push the elbow joint the wrong way with your hands or another part of the body.

CROSS ARMLOCK
(juji-gatame)

When your partner is curled up in the 'turtle' position, climb on her back and hook your feet underneath. Reach across her head with your left hand to scoop up her right arm.

Bring your left knee across the back of her neck to stop her crawling forward. Roll on to your shoulder and grab her trouser leg.

Patterns
(kata)

Judo has seven *katas*, or patterns, each of which consists of a series of movements.

Two partners work together to demonstrate their mastery of the techniques of judo in *kata* competitions.

1ST *KATA* (nage-no-kata)

The *kata* of throws was designed by Jigoro Kano. It is composed of 15 throws, grouped into five series of three movements. All judo tournaments should be opened by a demonstration of the *nage-no-kata*.

Blocking her head with your knee, roll over your shoulder and on to your back. Heave her legs across your body, rolling her over her own head. Use your right leg to help push.

With your left leg across her throat and your right leg across her chest, pull her arm out and push your hips up against her elbow to apply the armlock.

The cross armlock can be done in a variety of ways, even on a standing opponent, as Britain's Jamie Johnson proves here.

4TH KATA (kime-no-kata)
This ancient *kata* uses a variety of locks, strangles and strikes, sometimes against weapons.

7TH KATA (koshiki-no-kata)
This ancient *kata* simulates the battles of Japanese warriors, who fought wearing body armour.

THE SEVEN *KATAS* OF JUDO

1 *Nage-no-kata* – kata of throws
2 *Katame-no-kata* – kata on the ground
3 *Gonosen-no-kata* – kata of counters
4 *Kime-no-kata* – kata of self-defence
5 *Itsutsu-no-kata* – kata of the five principles
6 *Ju-no-kata* – kata of suppleness
7 *Koshiki-no-kata* – ancient *kata*

Useful information

If you want to find out more about judo or locate a club near you, the following organizations should be able to help.

INTERNATIONAL JUDO FEDERATION

www.ijf.org

BRITISH JUDO ASSOCIATION

www.britishjudo.org.uk

THE WORLD OF JUDO MAGAZINE

www.twoj.org

JUDO FEDERATION OF AUSTRALIA

www.ausport.gov.au/judo

All the Internet addresses (URLs) given in this book were valid at the time of going to press. However, due to the dynamic nature of the Internet, some addresses may have changed, or sites may have ceased to exist since publication. While the authors and publishers regret any inconvenience this may cause readers, no responsibility for any such changes can be accepted by either the authors or the publishers.

Useful addresses:
BRITISH JUDO ASSOCIATION
7a Rutland Street,
Leicester,
LE1 1RB
Tel: 01162 559669

THE WORLD OF JUDO
La Guerite,
Great George Street,
Bristol,
BS1 5QT
Tel: 01179 226270

JUDO FEDERATION OF AUSTRALIA
PO Box 919,
Glebe,
NSW 2037
Tel: 00 61 29 566 2063

Judo terms

ashi-waza foot sweeps
dan black belt grades
de-ashi-barai advanced
  foot sweep
dojo judo hall
gonosen-no-kata 3rd kata
hadaka-jime naked choke
ippon maximum knockout score
itsutsu-no-kata 5th kata
jigotai defensive posture
judogi judo uniform
judoka someone who
  practises judo
juji-gatame cross armlock
ju-no-kata 6th kata
kansetsu-waza armlocks
kata patterns
kata-gatame shoulder hold
katame-no-kata 2nd kata
kesa-gatame scarf hold
kime-no-kata 4th kata
koshiki-no-kata 7th kata
koshi-guruma hip wheel
koshi-waza hip throws
kumi-kata grip fighting
kyu senior grades below
  black belt

mon junior grades
nage-no-kata 1st kata
nage-waza throwing techniques
obi judo belt
okuri-eri-jime sliding
  collar choke
osaekomi-waza holding or
  pinning techniques
o-uchi-gari major inner sweep
randori free practice
rei bow
shime-waza strangulation
  technique
sutemi-waza sacrificial throw
tai-otoshi body drop
tani-otoshi valley drop
tatami judo mats
te waza hand techniques
tomoe-nage stomach throw
tori one who attacks or wins
uchi-komi technique practice
uchi-mata inner thigh throw
uke one who submits or defends
ukemi breakfalls
uki-goshi floating hip throw
uki-otoshi floating drop
yuko small score

Index